The Professor's Book of Whimsy

Published by Michael C Petty
www.petty.org.uk

Cover and Illustrations by Brenda Nash
www.brendanash.co.uk
Design by Robert Simpson
www.squirclecreative.co.uk
First Printing, 2018

British Library Cataloguing-in-Publication Data
A catalogue record for this book is available from the British Library

ISBN (Hardback) 978-1-9996039-0-8
ISBN (Paperback) 978-1-9996039-1-5
ISBN (E-Book) 978-1-9996039-2-2

Published by Michael C Petty
www.petty.org.uk

For Katie

CONTENTS

PREFACE

"It's funny because it's true."

If we are looking for an insight into humour, this is a good starting point. The account of Professor Stephen Hawking's party for time travellers is so bizarre that it must be genuine. Pranks on April 1st are invariably based on events that are plausible; our everyday experience then misleads us. But, we are also attracted to fantastic stories that are clearly untrue: snakes with spectacles, talking dogs, infuriating parrots.

There have been countless academic attempts to explain why we laugh. Like the blind men's descriptions of the elephant, most of these are only partially right.

Philosophers, in particular, have had a good stab at the subject. Plato, an influential critic of humour, treated it as an emotion that overrides rational self-control. There's the superiority theory, where contempt and derision produce laughter for the masses, but shame and embarrassment for an unlucky few. Ridicule and satire remain powerful focuses for humour. The 'UKIP members are not stupid' story illustrates this; the joke can, of course, be refocused on other political, religious or ethnic groups. There are the incongruity ideas (Kant and Schopenhauer) that suggest humour occurs when there is an incompatibility between what we expect and what actually occurs, as in the 'obituary for a farmer's wife.' The violation theory claims that we laugh when something is violated (social codes, linguistic norms or personal dignity); Dave Allen's 'room eight' is a very witty example. Freud naturally thought that mirth and laughter were reactions we produce in order to release sexual or aggressive tension.

Humour surely must serve an evolutionary purpose. Undoubtedly, laugher makes us happy and is a very sociable activity. To make sense of the world, we sometimes draw conclusions or make decisions in haste; humour helps us to identify such mistakes. So, it is no coincidence that good humour reflects real life. Comedy writers aspire to this. Shakespeare's A Midsummer Night's Dream is packed with eccentric players, but the magic in the play makes the characters even more outrageous. Bottom, for example, ends up with the head of an ass (unlike the Maid from Madras). Ray Galton and Alan Simpson were masters of their profession. Who else could lampoon John Osborne's Look Back in Anger so effectively with an entry in the East Cheam Drama Festival (starring the Lad himself)? The comedy show Steptoe and Son provides telling insights into inter-generational conflict.

Most of the jokes and stories in this book can be associated with one or more of the ideas above. But don't dwell on this. Jokes, like poetry, contain a certain structure, a natural rhythm, which make them appealing. This is often referred to as the rule-of-three: setup, reinforcement and punch line. The first two build tension, while the third releases anxiety, either through resolution or a twist. The setup is the foundation for most jokes. The process of creating a joke normally starts with finding a way in which two things or concepts are related. Once a connection is established, the setup usually needs to reinforce that connection. Concealment is sometimes required; otherwise the joke is too obvious. The concealment provides misdirection and confusion. Finally, the punch line creates the surprise; the release of tension necessary to get the laugh. Or, in the case of the 'man walked into a baker's shop' yarn, to ensure that confusion lingers. The tempo of jokes is obvious in the five-line limericks with a rhyme scheme AABBA and the rule of three is evident in the 'man walked into a bar' jokes. Even 'shaggy dog' stories conform to this linguistic pattern, although the reinforcement aspect is deliberately laboured.

What's so mysterious about the number three? It's no accident that the figure is pervasive throughout some of our greatest stories, fairy tales and myths. This is because knowledge presented in groups of three sticks in our heads better than other clusters of items: 'Friends, Romans, Countrymen,' 'Blood, Sweat and Tears,' 'Stop, Look and Listen,' 'Sex, Lies and Videotape.' It all comes down to the way we humans process information. By necessity, we have become proficient at pattern recognition, and three is the smallest number of elements required to create a pattern.

Here are some of my favourite jokes, stories and pranks, sprinkled with allegory, satire and parody. I have assembled everything under the whimsy umbrella, to suggest a more gentle and reflective style of humour than encountered in many joke compilations. My inspiration is taken from my background in science and academia; both fields of endeavour are rich and fertile sources of humour. Why have I included the conundrums? It is because these have a similar pattern and rhythm to the jokes. And they also possess the capacity to surprise.

Michael C Petty
County Durham, UK
June 2018

INTRODUCTION

Welcome to the latest innovation in communication, a new Bio-Optic Organised Knowledge device, which has been given the trade name BOOK™.

BOOK™ is a revolutionary breakthrough in technology; no batteries, no wires, no electric circuits; nothing to be connected or switched on. It's so easy to use that even a child can work it. It can be operated anywhere – even sitting in an armchair by the fire – yet it is powerful enough to hold as much information as a CD-ROM disc.

Here's how it works: BOOK™ is constructed of sequentially numbered sheets of paper (recyclable), each capable of holding thousands of 'bits' of information. This Paper Amalgam of General Encryption System is known as PAGES™. PAGES™ are locked together with a custom-fit device called a Binder, which ensures the sheets are kept in their correct sequence indefinitely. Opaque Paper Technology (OPT) allows manufacturers to use both sides of each sheet, doubling the information density and cutting costs. Experts are divided about the prospects for more increases in information density, but for now, BOOKS™ containing more information simply use more PAGES™. Each sheet is scanned using a standard Mark 1 Eyeball, which registers information directly into the user's brain without the need for any additional interface device. A flick of the finger allows scanning of the next sheet.

BOOK™ may be taken up at any time and is rendered operational by simply opening it. BOOK™ never crashes or requires rebooting, although, like other display devices, it can be rendered unusable by prolonged immersion in water. The 'Browse' feature, which is built in at no extra cost, allows the user to move instantly to any sheet and backwards and forwards as required. Many come with an 'Index' accessory that pinpoints the exact location of any selected material for instant retrieval.

An optional 'BOOK™-mark' add-on allows the user to open BOOK™ at the exact place at which the previous session was terminated – even if the BOOK™ has been closed in the interim! BOOK™-marks fit universal design standards; thus a single BOOK™-mark can be used in a BOOK™ produced by any manufacturer. Conversely, numerous BOOK™-marks can be used in a single BOOK™ if the user wishes to store several views at once – only the number of PAGES™ in the BOOK™ limits the number. You can also make personal notes next to BOOK™ text entries using one or more of the operational programming tools, the Portable Erasable Nib Cryptic Intercommunication Language Stylus (PENCILS™).

Portable, durable and affordable, BOOK™ is being hailed as the precursor of a new entertainment wave. The appeal of BOOK™ appears so certain that thousands of content-creators have committed to the platform and significant investment has already been made in their production. BOOK™ is such a versatile product that specialist shops are expected to appear in every high street to sell them.

If you are impressed with this example, find your nearest BOOK™-seller as soon as you can!

WONDERS OF SCIENCE

New Discovery

Physicists recently discovered the heaviest element known to science. Tentatively named Administratium, the element has no protons or electrons, so its atomic number is 0. However, it does have one neutron, 87 assistant neutrons, 75 vice-neutrons, 38 associate vice-neutrons and 111 assistant vice-neutrons. This gives it an atomic mass of 312. A force that involves meson-like particles, called morons, holds these 312 particles together.

Because it has no protons or electrons, Administratium is inert. Nonetheless, it can be detected chemically, because it impedes every reaction at which it is present. According to one of the discoverers, just a small amount of Administratium made a reaction that normally lasts less than one second take more than four days.

Administratium has a half-life of approximately three years. It does not actually decay; instead, it undergoes a reorganisation in which vice-neutrons, assistant neutrons and certain assistants to the neutrons exchange places. Some studies have indicated that its mass actually increases after each reorganisation, although this has yet to be explained. Another phenomenon that has been observed (as expected from quantum mechanics) is that the more one tries to pin down the positions of the vice-neutrons within the structure of Administratium, the more uncertain those positions become.

Administratium is known to be toxic and may be a serious hazard in the workplace. It is commonly found in an institution's newest, best-appointed and best-maintained buildings. Toxicologists report that there is no case known in which Administratium was cleansed from such a setting once it accumulated there.

Different Opinions

A mathematician, a biologist and a physicist are sitting in a café, watching people coming and going from a house opposite.

First, they see two people going into the house.

Time passes. They then notice three people coming out of the house.

The physicist says, "*The initial observation wasn't accurate.*"

The biologist says, "*They have reproduced.*"

The mathematician says, "*If exactly one person enters the house, then it will be empty again.*"

Black Sheep

An astronomer, a physicist and a mathematician were holidaying in Scotland. Through a train window, they observed a black sheep in the middle of a field.

"*How interesting,*" noted the astronomer, "*all Scottish sheep are black!*"

To which the physicist responded, "*No, no! Some Scottish sheep are black!*"

The mathematician gazed skyward in despair, and then said, "*In Scotland, there exists at least one field, containing at least one sheep, at least one side of which is black.*"

More Sheep

An engineer, a physicist and a mathematician are shown a field with a flock of sheep. They are told to put the sheep inside the smallest possible amount of fence.

The engineer is first. She herds the sheep into a circle and then puts the fence around them, declaring, "*A circle will use the least fence for a given area, so this is the best solution.*"

The physicist is next. She creates a circular fence of infinite radius around the sheep and then draws the fence tight around the flock, declaring, "*This will give the smallest circular fence around the herd.*"

Finally, it is the turn of the mathematician. After giving the problem a little thought, he puts a small fence around himself and states, "*I define myself to be on the outside!*"

What Scientists Say in Their Publications and What They Mean

It has long been known that	I didn't look up the original reference
A definite trend is evident	The data are practically meaningless
Three of the samples were chosen for detailed study	The other results didn't make any sense
Typical results are shown	The best results are shown
Careful statistical analysis	After going through a dozen books, we finally found one obscure test that we could apply
Correct to within an order of magnitude	Wrong
...accidentally strained during mounting	...dropped on the floor
...handled with extreme care	...not dropped on the floor
The agreement with the predicted curve is excellent	fair
good	poor
satisfactory	doubtful
fair	imaginary
as good as could be expected	non-existent
It is suggested that... It is believed that... It may be that...	I think
Thanks are due to Joe Smith for assistance with the experiments and Anne Jones for valuable discussions	Smith did the work and Jones explained what it meant

Back to the Drawing Board

When NASA first started sending astronauts into space, they quickly discovered that ballpoint pens would not work in zero gravity. To combat the problem, NASA scientists spent a decade and $12 billion on developing a pen that could write in zero gravity, upside down, underwater, on almost any surface including glass and at temperatures ranging from below freezing to 300 °C.

The Russians, on the other hand, used a pencil.

Time Travel

To test if time travel is feasible, in 2009, Professor Stephen Hawking threw a champagne party for time travellers – complete with Krug champagne and hors d'oeuvres. He didn't send out the invitations until after the party had taken place. If people had shown up, he hypothesised, it would be proof that time travel is possible. Since nobody came, time travel is not real – probably.

On Average

A doctor, a lawyer, and a statistician are out hunting. They see a deer. The doctor takes the first shot and shoots five feet to the left. The lawyer takes the second shot and shoots five feet to the right. The statistician simply notes, "*We got 'im!*"

Folk Law

In autumn, the Indians on a remote reservation in South Dakota asked their new chief if the coming winter was going to be cold or mild.

Since he was a chief in a modern society, he had never been taught the old secrets. So, when he looked up at the sky, he couldn't tell what the winter was going to be like.

Nevertheless, to be on the safe side, he told his tribe that the winter was indeed going to be cold and that the members of the village should collect firewood to be prepared.

But, being a pragmatic person, he had an idea. He went to the local phone box, called the National Weather Service and asked, *"Is the coming winter going to be cold?"*

"It looks like this winter is going to be quite cold," the meteorologist at the Weather Service responded.

So, the chief went back to his people and told them to collect even more firewood in order to be prepared.

A week later, he called the National Weather Service again. *"Does it still look like it is going to be a very cold winter?"*

"Yes," the man at Weather Service again replied, *"it's going to be a very cold winter."*

The chief again went back to his people and ordered them to collect every scrap of firewood they could find.

Two weeks later, the chief called the National Weather Service again. *"Are you absolutely certain that the winter is going to be very cold?"*

"Absolutely," the man replied. *"It's looking more and more like it is going to be one of the coldest winters we've ever seen."*

"How can you be so sure?" the chief enquired.

The weatherman replied, *"The Indians up your way are stockpiling firewood."*

Funny Calculus

$$\int \frac{1}{\text{cabin}}\, d(\text{cabin}) = \log \text{cabin} + c = \text{houseboat}$$

Does Santa Exist?

Here are some thoughts:

No known species of reindeer can fly. But, there are 300,000 species of living organisms yet to be classified, and while most of these are insects and microorganisms, this does not completely rule out flying reindeer.

There are about two billion children in the world. However, since Santa doesn't (appear to) visit the Muslim, Hindu, Jewish and Buddhist children, this reduces the workload to 15% of the total. On an estimate of 3.5 children per household, that's about 90 million homes. One presumes there's at least one good child in each.

Santa has 31 hours of Christmas to work with, thanks to the different time zones and the rotation of the earth, assuming he travels east to west (which seems logical). This works out at about 800 visits per second. This is to say that, for each Christian household with good children, Santa has approximately 1/1000th of a second to park, hop out of the sleigh, work his way jump down the chimney, fill the stockings, distribute the remaining presents under the tree, eat whatever snacks have been left, climb the chimney, get back into the sleigh and move on to the next house. Assuming that each of these 90 million stops are evenly distributed around the earth (dubious), we are now talking about 0.8 miles per household, a total trip of about 70 million miles, not counting stops to do what most of us must do at least once every 31 hours, plus feeding etc. This means that Santa's sleigh is moving at 650 miles per second – 3,000 times the speed of sound. For purposes of comparison, the fastest man-made vehicle on earth (2016), the Juno space probe, moves at a sluggish 45.8 miles per second. And a normal reindeer can run 15 miles per hour at the most.

The cargo on the sleigh adds another interesting factor. Assuming that each child gets nothing more than a medium-sized Lego set (2 pounds), the sleigh is carrying 321,300 tons, not counting Santa, who is invariably described as overweight. On land, conventional reindeer can pull no more than 300 pounds. Even granting that 'flying reindeer' (see first point above) could pull ten times the normal amount, we cannot do the job with eight, or even nine. We would need 214,200 reindeer. This increases the payload – not even counting the weight of the sleigh – to 353,430 tons. Again, for comparison – this is four times the weight of the Queen Elizabeth.

353,000 tons travelling at 650 miles per second creates enormous air resistance – this will heat the reindeer up in the same manner as a spacecraft re-entering the earth's atmosphere. The lead pair of reindeer will absorb 14.3 quintillion (ten raised to the power of eighteen) joules of energy each, per second.

In short, they will burst into flame almost instantaneously, exposing the reindeer behind them, and create deafening sonic booms in their wake. The entire reindeer team will be vaporised within four thousandths of a second. Santa, meanwhile, will be subjected to centrifugal forces 18,000 times greater than gravity. A 250-pound Santa (which seems ludicrously slim) would be pinned to the back of his sleigh by over four million pounds of force.

In conclusion – if Santa ever did attempt to deliver presents on Christmas Eve, he didn't get very far.

Marital Malfunction

From: Polly Estor, Chemistry Department
To: Arthur Bight, Computer Support
Subject: Failed Upgrade

Last year I upgraded from Boyfriend 7.0 to Husband 1.0 and noticed that the new program began unexpected 3F (football, fishing and flatulence) processing that took up a lot of space and valuable resources. No mention of this phenomenon was included in the supporting documentation. In addition, Husband 1.0 installs itself into all other programs and launches during system initialisation, where it monitors all other system activity. Applications such as Pilates 10.3, Shopping 2.5 and Spanish Lessons 5.0 no longer run, crashing the system whenever selected. I cannot keep Husband 1.0 in the background while attempting to run some of my other favourite applications like Girls Night Out 4.3, Book Club 2.0 and Art Gallery 7.77. I am thinking about going back to Boyfriend 7.0, but the uninstall does not work on this program. I tried to uninstall Husband 1.0 but got this error: 'General Protection Fault in module House Security. The Uninstallation will abort.' Can you help me, please?

From: Arthur Bight, Computer Support
To: Polly Estor, Chemistry Department
Re: Failed Upgrade

This is a very common problem among women, but it is due mostly to a primary misconception. Many upgrade from Boyfriend 7.0 to Husband 1.0 with the idea that Husband 1.0 is merely a UTILITIES & ENTERTAINMENT program. Husband 1.0 is actually an OPERATING SYSTEM and designed by its programmer to run everything. It is unlikely you would be able to purge Husband 1.0 and still convert back to Boyfriend 7.0. It is impossible to uninstall, delete or purge Husband 1.0 from the system once installed. You cannot go back to Boyfriend 7.0 because Husband 1.0 is not designed to do this. Some have tried to install Boyfriend 8.0 or Husband 2.0 but end up with more problems than the original system. Look in your manual under 'Warnings – Divorce/Child Support;' this was given to you at time of registration with Husband 1.0.

I recommend you keep Husband 1.0 and just deal with the situation. I might also suggest you read the entire section regarding General Partnership Faults (GPFs). The best course of action will be to enter the command C:\COMPROMISE. In fact, I would suggest you use this command every time Husband 1.0 crashes on your system. Husband 1.0 is a great program, but very high maintenance. Consider buying additional software to improve the performance of Husband 1.0. I recommend Golfing Holiday 2.1, Barbeque 5.0 or Trip to Pub 4.5. Do not, under any circumstances, install Personal Fitness Instructor with Six-Pack 3.3. This is not a supported application for Husband 1.0 and is likely to cause irreversible damage to the operating system. Recent surveys show add-ons like Sexy Dress 2.0, Science Fiction Films 3.0 and Classic Car 1.0 are the best Third-Party tools supported by Husband 1.0 to allow it to run smoothly and effectively.

Best of luck!

Better Safe than Sorry

When a statistician passes the airport security check, a bomb is found in his bag. He explains, "*Statistics show that the probability of a bomb being on an aeroplane is 1/1000. However, the chance that there are two bombs on one plane is 1/1000000. So, I am much safer...*"

Conundrum A

A Geordie teacher has two boyfriends, one in North Shields and one in Central Newcastle. She lives in Wallsend and uses the local Metro station to visit her friends. Since she likes both men equally, she simply takes the first train that comes along. In this way, she uses chance to determine who she should visit. The lass reaches Wallsend Metro at a random time each Saturday afternoon. Newcastle and North Shields trains arrive at the station equally often – every ten minutes. Yet, the girl finds herself spending most of her time in North Shields; in fact, on average she goes there nine times out of ten. Why?

WIT AND WISDOM

Lateral Thinking

The owner of a local hardware shop is dismayed when a huge new DIY centre opens up next door, erecting large sign saying, 'Best Deals.' He is even more horrified when another large DIY store opens on the other side of his shop, putting up an even larger sign saying, 'Lowest Prices.' After the panic has abated, the shop owner has a bright idea. He puts a large sign over his own shop, stating, 'Main Entrance.'

Much, Much More Important Than That

It's the FA Cup Final, and a man makes his way to his seat, right next to the pitch. He sits down, noticing that the seat next to him is empty. He leans over and asks his neighbour if someone will be sitting there. "*No,*" says the neighbour. "*The seat is empty.*"

"*This is incredible,*" says the man. "*Who in their right mind would have a seat like this for the Final and not use it?*"

The neighbour says, "*Well, actually, the seat belongs to me. I was supposed to come with my wife, but she passed away. This is the first Cup Final we haven't been to together since we got married."*

"Oh, I'm so sorry to hear that. That's terrible...but couldn't you find someone else, a friend, relative or even a neighbour to take her seat?"

The man shakes his head. "*No,*" he says. "*They're all at the funeral.*"

On Overcharging

A woman takes her duck to the vet. He says, "*I'm sorry, but it's dead.*"

She says, "*I don't believe it.*"

The vet calls in a Labrador. The dog sniffs the body of the duck, lowers its head dolefully, shakes it left to right and walks out. Then, in comes a cat. He licks the duck, lowers his head, gives a sad nod and leaves.

The vet announces, "*That'll be £1,000.*"

The lady responds, "*But that's outrageous.*"

The vet says, "*It would have been £200, but you've got to add the lab report and the cat scan.*"

More Overcharging

A woman calls in a plumber when her washing machine breaks down. The plumber arrives, studies the machine, then produces a hammer and gives it a hefty whack. The washing machine starts working again and the plumber presents a bill for £200. "*Two hundred pounds?*" says the woman. "*All you did was hit it with a hammer.*" So the plumber then produces an itemised bill:

'Hitting washing machine with hammer – £5.

Knowing where to hit it – £195.'

BANG
'EM
'ARD
ELECTRICS
OW!

Human Sacrifice

Two men are out for a walk in the forest when they see a bear. The first takes off his backpack, pulls out a pair of trainers and puts them on. The other looks at him and says, "*That's stupid. You can't outrun a bear!*"

"*That's true,*" says his friend. "*But then again, I only need to outrun you.*"

Dress Code

A man goes into a nightclub wearing a shirt open at the collar. A bouncer refuses him entry, as he is not wearing a tie. So, the man goes back to his car to look for a tie. Unfortunately, he doesn't have one. But, he sees a set of jump leads in the boot. In desperation, he ties these around his neck, manages to fashion a fairly acceptable-looking knot and lets the ends dangle free. He returns to the nightclub. The bouncer looks him over for a few minutes and then says, "*Well, OK, I guess you can come in. Just don't start anything.*"

Job for Life

A young lad enters a barber's shop and the barber whispers to his customer, "*This is the dimmest boy in the world. Watch while I prove it to you.*" The barber puts a five-pound note in one hand and two pound coins in the other, then calls the boy over and asks, "*Which do you want, Tom?*" The boy takes the pound coins and leaves. "*What did I tell you?*" said the barber. "*That lad never learns!*"

Later, when the customer leaves, he sees Tom coming out of an ice cream shop. "*Hey there! May I ask you a question? Why did you take the pound coins instead of the five-pound note?*" Tom licked his cone and replied, "*Because the day I take the note, the game is over!*"

One Step Ahead

Three engineers and three accountants are travelling by train to a conference. At the station, the three accountants watch as the three engineers buy only a single ticket.

"*How are three people going to travel on only one ticket?*" asks an accountant.

"*Watch and you'll see,*" answers an engineer.

They all board the train. The accountants take their respective seats, but all three engineers cram into the toilet and close the door behind them.

Shortly after the train has departed, the conductor comes around collecting tickets. He knocks on the toilet door and says, "*Ticket, please.*" The door opens just a crack and a single arm emerges with a ticket in hand. The conductor takes it and moves on. The accountants see this and agree it is a clever idea. So after the conference, the accountants decide to copy the engineers on the return trip and save some money. When they arrive at the station, they buy a single ticket for the return trip.

To their astonishment, the engineers don't buy a ticket at all. "*How are you going to travel without a ticket?*" asks one perplexed accountant.

"*Watch and you'll see,*" responds an engineer.

When they board the train, the three accountants cram into a toilet and the three engineers cram into another one nearby. The train departs.

Shortly afterwards, one of the engineers leaves his toilet and walks over to the toilet where the accountants are hiding. He knocks on the door and says. "*Ticket, please.*"

Catch-22

A man walks into a baker's shop and asks for a loaf of bread. The baker asks, "*Do you want white or brown?*"

The man replies, "*It doesn't matter – I've got my bike outside.*"

Dead Cert

A man buys a donkey from an old farmer for £100. The farmer agrees to deliver the donkey the next day.

When the farmer arrives, he says, "*Sorry, but I have some bad news for you. The donkey has died.*"

"*Well then, just refund my money,*" says the man.

"*Can't do that,*" responds the farmer. "*I've gone and spent it.*"

"*OK,*" says the man. "*Unload the donkey.*"

"*What will you do with him?*" asks the farmer.

"*I shall raffle him off.*"

"*But you can't raffle a dead donkey!*"

"*Oh, yes I can, just watch. I just won't tell anyone he's dead.*"

A month later, the farmer and the man meet up.

"*What happened with the dead donkey?*" enquires the farmer.

"*I raffled him off,*" replies the man. "*I sold 500 tickets at £2 each and made a profit of £898.*"

"*Didn't anyone complain?*"

"*Just the guy who won. So, I gave him back his £2.*"

BON

Old Bill

An old man lived alone on the North Yorkshire Moors. He wanted to dig his garden to plant a potato crop, but it was very hard work. His only son, who would have helped him, was in prison for bank robbery. The old man wrote a letter to his son and mentioned his predicament. Shortly, he received this reply: "*For heavens' sake Dad, don't dig up that garden, that's where I buried the money!*"

At 4 am the next morning, a dozen policemen turn up and dig over the entire garden, without finding any money. Confused, the old man writes another note to his son, telling him what happened and asking him what to do next. His son's reply: "*Now plant your potatoes, Dad.*"

Conundrum B

The College Dean wants to give a very small dinner party. He means to ask his father's brother-in-law, his brother's father-in-law, his father-in-law's brother and his brother-in-law's father. How many guests are there if the dinner party is to be as small as possible?

Q & A

Q. How many professors does it take to screw in a light bulb?

A. Just one – he holds the bulb up to the socket and waits for the world to revolve around him.

Q. What is the difference between a sperm and a university inspector?

A. A sperm has a million to one chance of becoming human.

Q. What's the difference between an etymologist and an entomologist?

A. An etymologist knows the difference.

Q. Why does a hamburger have less entropy than a steak?

A. Because it's in the ground state.

Q. What's round and bad-tempered?

A. A vicious circle.

Q. What is the relationship between a doormat and a doorstep?

A. A stepfather.

Q. What is the best invention to date?
A. The venetian blind – otherwise it would have been curtains for all of us.

Q. What is the common name of the molecule CH2O?
A. Seawater.

Q. What is the formula for the volume of a thick crust pizza with height 'a' and radius 'z'?
A. Pizza.

Q. Why can you never trust atoms?
A. They make up everything!

Q. Why did the chicken cross the Möbius strip?
A. To get to the same side.

Q. Why did the computer programmer always confuse Halloween with Christmas?
A. Because OCT 31 = DEC 25.

Conundrum C

Two players are seated at a square table. The first player places a coin on the table, the second places a coin on the table, and they carry on placing coins one after another, with the only condition that the coins are not allowed to touch. The winner is the person who places the final coin on the table, meaning that he or she fills the last remaining space between the other coins.

The table must be larger than a single coin and all the coins placed must be identical.

One player is always guaranteed to win. Which is it – the one who starts or the one who goes second? And what is his or her winning strategy?

ANIMAL MAGIC

The Lion and Albert

The following monologue, written by Marriott Edgar (designed to be spoken with piano accompaniment), was originally published during the 1930s. (To be read out loud in a Lancashire accent…)

There's a famous seaside place called Blackpool,
That's noted for fresh air and fun,
And Mr and Mrs Ramsbottom
Went there with young Albert, their son.

A grand little lad was young Albert,
All dressed in his best; quite a swell
With a stick with an 'orse's 'ead 'andle,
The finest that Woolworth's could sell.

They didn't think much to the Ocean:
The waves, they were fiddlin' and small,
There was no wrecks and nobody drownded,
Fact, nothing to laugh at, at all.

So, seeking for further amusement,
They paid and went into the zoo,
Where they'd lions and tigers and camels,
And old ale and sandwiches too.

There were one great big lion called Wallace;
His nose were all covered with scars –
He lay in a somnolent posture,
With the side of his face on the bars.

Now Albert had heard about lions,
How they was ferocious and wild –
To see Wallace lying so peaceful,
Well, it didn't seem right to the child.

So straight 'way the brave little feller,
Not showing a morsel of fear,
Took his stick with its 'orse's 'ead 'andle
...And shoved it in Wallace's ear.

You could see the lion didn't like it,
For giving a kind of a roll,
He pulled Albert inside the cage with 'im,
And swallowed the little lad 'ole.

Then Pa, who had seen the occurrence,
And didn't know what to do next,
Said "*Mother! Yon lions 'et Albert,*"
And Mother said, "*Well, I am vexed!*"

Then Mr and Mrs Ramsbottom –
Quite rightly, when all's said and done –
Complained to the Animal Keeper,
That the lion had eaten their son.

The keeper was quite nice about it
He said "*What a nasty mishap*
Are you sure it's your boy he's eaten?"
Pa said "*Am I sure? There's his cap!*"

The manager had to be sent for.
He came and he said "*What's to do?*"
Pa said "*Yon lion's 'et Albert,*
And 'im in his Sunday clothes, too."

Then Mother said, "*Right's right, young feller;*
I think it's a shame and a sin,
For a lion to go and eat Albert,
And after we've paid to come in."

The manager wanted no trouble,
He took out his purse right away,
Saying "*How much to settle the matter?*"
And Pa said "*What do you usually pay?*"

But Mother had turned a bit awkward
When she thought where her Albert had gone
She said "*No! someone's got to be summonsed*" –
So that was decided upon.

Then off they went to the P'lice Station
In front of the Magistrate chap;
They told 'im what happened to Albert,
And proved it by showing his cap.

The Magistrate gave his opinion
That no one was really to blame
And he said that he hoped the Ramsbottoms
Would have further sons to their name.

At that Mother got proper blazing,
"*And thank you, sir, kindly,*" said she.
"What waste all our lives raising children
To feed ruddy lions? Not me!"

Shaggy Dog

There were three kingdoms, each bordering the same lake. For centuries, these kingdoms had fought over an island in the middle of the lake. One day, they decided to have it out, once and for all. The first kingdom was quite rich, and sent an army of 25 knights, each with three squires. The night before the battle, the knights jousted and cavorted as their squires polished armour, cooked food and sharpened weapons.

The second kingdom was not so wealthy, and sent only ten knights, each with two squires. The night before the battle, the knights cavorted and sharpened their weapons as the squires polished armour and prepared dinner.

The third kingdom was very poor, and only sent one elderly knight with his sole squire. The night before the battle, the knight sharpened his weapon, while the squire, using a looped rope, slung a pot high over the fire to cook while he prepared the knight's armour.

The next day, the battle began. All the knights of the first two kingdoms had cavorted a bit too much (one should never cavort while sharpening weapons and jousting) and could not fight. The squire of the third kingdom could not rouse the elderly knight in time for combat. So, in the absence of the knights, the squires fought.

The battle raged well into the late hours, but when the dust finally settled, a solitary figure limped from the carnage. The lone squire from the third kingdom dragged himself away, beaten, bloodied, but victorious.

And it just goes to prove, the squire of the high pot and noose is equal to the sum of the squires of the other two sides.

Now You See It

A magician was working on a cruise ship. Since the audience was different each week, the magician did the same tricks over and over again.

There was only one problem: the Captain's parrot saw the shows each week and began to understand how the magician did every trick. Once he understood, he started shouting in the middle of the show, "*Look, it's not the same hat!*" or, "*Look, he's hiding the flowers under the table!*" Or "*Hey, why are all the cards the ace of spades?"*

The magician was furious but couldn't do anything. It was, after all, the Captain's parrot.

Then one stormy night on the Pacific Ocean, the ship sank.

The magician, luckily, found himself on a piece of wood floating in the middle of the sea, as fate would have it...with the parrot.

They stared at each other with hatred, but did not utter a word.

This went on for a day...and then two days. And then three days. Finally, on the fourth day, the parrot could not hold back any longer and said...

"*Okay, I give up. What have you done with the ship?*"

Won't Take No for an Answer

One day, a duck walks into a shop and asks the manager if they sell grapes. The manager says, "*No, we don't sell grapes.*" The duck goes home and comes back the next day and asks the same question. The manager says the same thing again, "*No, we do not sell grapes.*" The duck goes home, comes back the next day and asks the manager if they sell grapes. This time the manager says, "*No, we don't sell grapes! If you ask one more time, I will nail your beak to the floor!*" The duck goes home. It comes back the next day and asks the manager if he has any nails. The manager says, "*No, I don't have any nails.*" The duck says, "*Okay, good. Do you sell grapes?*"

What's in a Name

Late one night, a burglar broke into a house and while he was sneaking around, he heard a voice say, "*Jesus is watching you.*" He looked around and saw nothing. He kept on creeping and again heard, "*Jesus is watching you.*" In a dark corner, he saw a cage with a parrot inside. The burglar asked the parrot, "*Was it you who said Jesus is watching me?*" The parrot replied, "*Yes.*" Relieved, the burglar asked, "*What is your name?*" The parrot said, "*Clarence.*" The burglar said, "*That's a stupid name for a parrot. What idiot named you Clarence?*" The parrot answered, "*The same idiot that named the Rottweiler Jesus.*"

A Dog's Life

Every night, a couple is kept awake by the barking of their next-door neighbour's dog. Finally, the man has had enough and jumps out of bed. "*Right!*" he says. "*I'm going to teach them a lesson.*" He runs downstairs and comes back five minutes later.

"*What did you do?*" asks his wife.

"*I've put their dog in our garden,*" replies the man. "*Let's see how they like it.*"

Value for Money

A man spots a sign outside a house that reads 'Talking Dog for Sale.' Intrigued, he walks in. "*So what have you done with your life?*" he asks the dog.

"*I've led a very full life,*" says the dog. "*I lived in the Alps, rescuing avalanche victims. Then I served my country in Iraq. And now I spend my days reading to the residents of a retirement home.*"

The man is flabbergasted. He asks the dog's owner, "*Why on earth would you want to get rid of an incredible dog like that?*"

The owner says, "*Because he's a liar! He never did any of that!*"

Conversation with the Cheshire Cat

(from Alice's Adventures in Wonderland by Lewis Carroll, Chapter 6)

"*But I don't want to go among mad people,*" Alice remarked.

"*Oh, you can't help that,*" said the Cat: "*we're all mad here. I'm mad. You're mad.*"

"*How do you know I'm mad?*" said Alice.

"*You must be,*" said the Cat, "*or you wouldn't have come here.*"

Mother Knows Best

The wise old Mother Superior was dying. The nuns gathered around her bed, trying to make her comfortable. They gave her some warm milk to drink, but she refused it.

Then one nun took the glass back to the kitchen. Remembering a bottle of whisky received as a gift the previous Christmas, she opened it and poured a generous amount into the warm milk.

Back at Mother Superior's bed, she held the glass to her lips. Mother drank a little, and then a little more; then before she knew it, she had drunk the entire glassful.

"*Mother, Mother*" the nuns cried, "*Give us some of your wisdom before you pass away.*"

Mother Superior raised herself in the bed with a pious look on her face and pointing out of the window, she said, "*Don't sell that cow.*"

How a cat decides whether to scratch on something

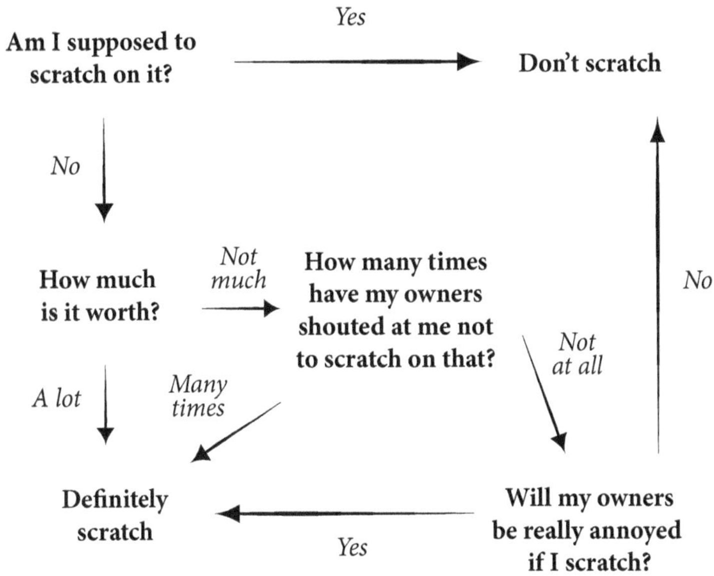

Conundrum D

The vicar asked the verger, "*How old are your three children?*"

The verger replied. "*If you add their ages, you get the number of my house. And if you multiply their ages together, you get 36.*"

The vicar went away for a while but then returned and told the verger that he could not solve the problem.

The verger told the vicar, "*Your son is older than any of my children,*" and added that the vicar would now be able to solve the problem.

What are the ages of the children?

THE ACADEMIC WORLD

Why God would never get an Academic Position

He only had one publication.

It was in Hebrew.

It had no references.

It wasn't published in a refereed journal.

Some even doubt he wrote it himself.

The scientific community had a hard time replicating his results.

He never applied to an Ethics Committee for permission to use human subjects.

When one experiment went awry, he covered it up by drowning the subjects.

He rarely came to class and instead told students to read the book.

Some say he arranged for his son to give the lectures.

Although there were only ten requirements, most students failed his tests.

Failing students were treated harshly.

It may be true that he created the world, but what has he done recently?

Conference Quandary

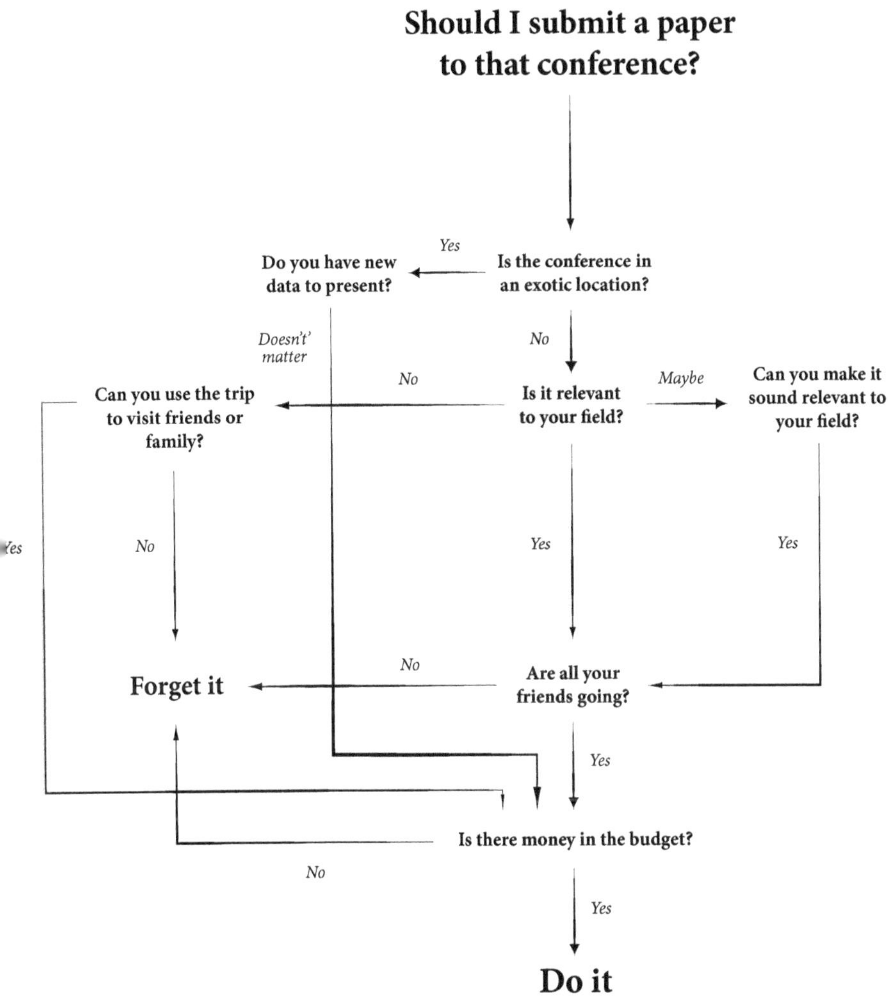

Leader's Lament

A woman is jogging through a park when she sees an old University Vice-Chancellor sitting on a bench sobbing. "*Can I help you?*" she asks. "*I don't think so,*" says the VC. "*My life is perfect. I'm incredibly rich, I just married a twenty-year-old model, I have a beautiful house with a pool and a private jet.*" "*So, why are you crying?*" asks the woman. The VC sobs, "*Because I can't remember where I live!*"

Means to an End

The following story, about a physics student who surprises his professor on a simple question of physics, was popularised by Alexander Calandra, Professor of Physics at Washington University. Calandra's essay entitled Angels on a Pin, appeared in his 1961 book, The Teaching of Elementary Science and Mathematics, Washington University Press. The story has been repeated numerous times. Legend has it that the student was Niels Bohr, recipient of the Nobel Prize of Physics in 1922. However, there is no evidence to support this.

A question on a university examination paper in physics asks: 'Describe how to determine the height of a skyscraper with a barometer.'

One student replied: "*You tie a long piece of string to the neck of the barometer, then lower the barometer from the roof of the skyscraper to the ground. The length of the string plus the length of the barometer will equal the height of the building.*"

This original answer so incensed the examiner that the student was failed. He appealed on the grounds that his answer was indisputably correct, and the university then appointed an independent external examiner to advise on the case.

The external examiner judged that the answer was indeed correct, but did not display any evidence of knowledge of physics.

To resolve the problem, it was decided that the student would be called and allowed ten minutes in which to provide a verbal answer that demonstrated his familiarity with the basic principles of physics.

For five minutes, the student sat in silence. The external reminded him that time was running out, to which the student replied that he had several extremely relevant answers, but couldn't make up his mind which to use.

On being advised to hurry up, the student replied:

"First, you could take the barometer up to the roof of the skyscraper, drop it over the edge and measure the time it takes to reach the ground. The height of the building can then be worked out from a simple formula. But bad luck on the barometer.

Or, if the sun is shining, you could measure the height of the barometer, then set it on end and measure the length of its shadow. Then you measure the length of the skyscraper's shadow. Thereafter, it is a simple matter of proportional arithmetic to work out the height of the skyscraper.

But if you wanted to be highly scientific about it, you could tie a short piece of string to the barometer and swing it like a pendulum, first at ground level and then on the roof of the skyscraper. The height is worked out by the difference in the gravitational restoring force.

Alternatively, if the skyscraper has an outside emergency staircase, it would be easier to walk up it and mark off the height of the skyscraper in barometer lengths, then add them up.

If you wanted a straightforward solution to the problem, you could use the barometer to measure the air pressure on the roof of the skyscraper and on the ground, and convert the difference in millibars into feet, to give the height of the building.

But since we are constantly being exhorted to exercise independence of mind and apply scientific methods, undoubtedly the best way would be to knock on the concierge's door and say to him 'Would you like a nice new barometer? I will give you this one if you tell me the height of this skyscraper.'"

Passing the Buck

The position of a University Head of Department usually rotates every three years.

In one University, the outgoing Head met privately with the new incumbent and handed him three numbered envelopes.

"*Open these if you run up against a problem you don't think you can solve,*" the former Head said.

Things progressed smoothly for the first six months, but then student numbers took a downturn and the new Head came under pressure from the Dean. He went to his drawer and took out the first envelope. The message read, 'Blame your predecessor.' The new Head then tactfully laid the blame at the feet of the previous holder of the office. The student intake picked up and the problem was soon behind him.

About a year later, the Department had performed badly in its research assessment. Having learned from his previous experience, the Head opened the second envelope. The message read, 'Reorganise.' This he did, and the Department quickly rebounded.

However, in the Head's third year of office, the Department once again fell on hard times. Both the student numbers and research grant income were plummeting.

The Head went to his office, closed the door and opened the third envelope.

The message said, 'Prepare three envelopes.'

Academic Venn Diagram

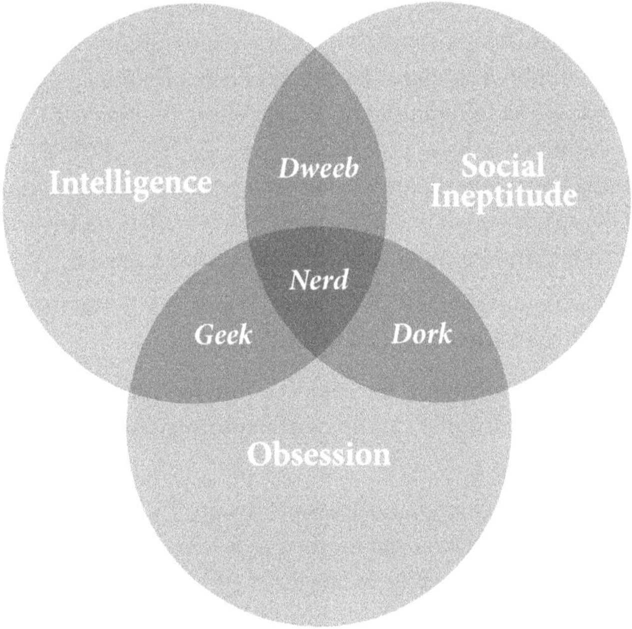

Big Bastard

The University of Pizza (The Fast Food University) is located in the North of England.

Now read on...

He couldn't sleep. The night was humid and the mattress felt like a sack of potatoes (Pentland Javelin, early crop). Thoughts of the last Research Review went through his head. Had it been wise to leave the submission to Old Gumbie? The Vice-Chancellor's chauffeur and odd job person had only achieved One Star, which paled into insignificance when compared to the Four-Star ratings obtained by Pizza's two southern rivals, the prestigious

Universities of Bucks and Fizz. The VC had never forgiven him. Following the withdrawal of the sponsorship of his Chair of Whimsy, his job was on the line. The future of Pizza's Philosophy Department hung in the balance. And what about teaching quality assessment, undergraduate questionnaires, staff salaries, tuition fees, appraisal, postgraduate recruitment? But, above all, how on earth did he find himself in this situation, imprisoned with Dr Iago from the University of Fizz (now snoring soundly from the bunk below) in a prefabricated house and surrounded by microphones and television cameras? Iago had the reputation of being the most Machiavellian and scheming academic in the country, so he knew he had his work cut out.

The call had come from the Vice-Chancellor earlier in the year – urgent and top priority. So he hastened to Old Pepperoni Hall.

"*Now then, Skimbleshanks,*" said the VC from the comfort of his new faux leather reclining chair (offer from Lloyds Bank on eBay), "*I have important work for you.*"

As a result of the tremendous success of Reality TV shows, the new academic channel Hot Dons had decided to orient such a series to the university world. This would be an amalgam of University Challenge and Big Brother – a kind of 'I'm A Professor, Get Me Out of Here.' Universities from all over the country would be asked to suggest names of suitable competitors. For the VC, this was a chance to rid him temporarily of the more problematic staff during the preparation of the next University Research Review, and, of course, save the odd salary for three months.

The competition was intense. Professor Blair (University of Wigan) had been ejected early on for being unable to recognise not only photographs of his tutorial group, but also those of his departmental colleagues. Dr Clemens (Huckleberry College) had come last in the Chair of Committee competition by failing to keep a meeting with a two-item agenda going for more than five hours, while Dr Dodgson (Queen's University) had brought disgrace and humiliation to his institution by not knowing the difference between an 'aim' and an 'objective.' This left only Skimbleshanks and the insidious Iago.

As Skimbleshanks dozed, he became aware of a disembodied voice, floating through the ether.

"*This is Big Bastard. Will Professor Skimbleshanks make his way to the Diary Room?*"

As soon as Skimbleshanks was seated, the voice continued.

"There will be one final test to determine the winner of Big Bastard. Listen carefully.

In a certain university, a slight 'problem' has occurred with some of the examination papers and the answers have been printed alongside the questions. The papers are individually sealed, so it is not possible to detect the 'forged' ones by inspection. However, the correct papers are known to weigh 5 grams each, while those papers printed with the answers weigh 20% more. There are ten piles of papers, each containing ten scripts; one of these piles comprises ten forged scripts while the other nine consist of correct scripts. You are provided with a single-pan electronic balance. What is the minimum number of separate weighings to be sure of locating the pile of bogus scripts?"

Dr Iago had already worked out that he could do it with six weighings. But, like all academics that had lost their way and relied on political manoeuvrings to secure their career, Iago had also lost the ability for rational thought. Skimbleshanks knew that he could complete the task with just one trip to the balance.

Skimbleshanks' triumph on his return to Pizza was complete. He was a Four-Star performer and there was no way that the Vice-Chancellor could send Skimbleshanks to his retirement now. But then, that was the curious thing. While Skimbleshanks had been away, the VC had announced his own retirement. The Deputy Vice-Chancellor had also gone to pastures new, which left the University temporarily in the hands of Ms Macavity, the Treasurer, assisted naturally by Old Gumbie.

"*Whatever next?*" mused Skimbleshanks.

Democracy Rules

The Dean is hospitalised after a heart attack. As he is lying in his hospital bed, reflecting on his near brush with death, a nurse arrives with a beautiful bouquet of flowers. The Dean asks the nurse to hand him the card, which reads, 'By a vote of 26 to three with two abstentions, the Faculty wish you a speedy recovery.'

Thinking at the Speed of Light

When Albert Einstein was making the rounds of the speakers' circuit, he usually found himself eagerly longing to get back to his scientific work.

One night, as they were driving to yet another event, Einstein mentioned to his chauffeur (a man who somewhat resembled Einstein in looks and manner) that he was tired of speechmaking.

"*I have an idea, boss,*" his chauffeur said. "*I've heard you give this speech so many times – I'll bet I could give it for you.*"

Einstein laughed loudly and said, "*Why not? Let's do it!*"

When they arrived, Einstein donned the chauffeur's cap and jacket and sat at the back of the room. The chauffeur gave a beautiful rendition of Einstein's speech and even answered a few questions expertly.

Then a pompous professor asked an extremely esoteric question about anti-matter formation, digressing here and there to let everyone in the audience know that he was nobody's fool. Without missing a beat, the chauffeur fixed the professor with a steely stare and said, "*Sir, the answer to that question is so simple that I will let my chauffeur, who is sitting in the back, answer it for me.*"

Touché

Two undergraduates were taking their chemistry finals. Both had done well enough in previous years to be assured of first-class degrees. The friends were so confident that they decided to go up to town and have a few beers with some chums the weekend before finals week, even though the organic chemistry exam was on Monday morning.

They had a great time. However, with their hangovers, they slept all day Sunday and didn't get back to campus until the Monday morning. Rather than taking their finals then, they went to see their professor after the exam had finished and explained to her why they had missed it. They told her that they went to town for the weekend and had planned to return in time to study, but had a puncture on the way back. They didn't have a spare wheel and couldn't get help for a very long time. Consequently, they were very late getting back to campus.

The professor thought this over and then agreed that they could take a revised examination the following day. The students were very relieved. They studied that night and went in the next day at the appointed time.

The professor placed the students in separate rooms, handed each of them a test paper and told them to begin. They looked at the first problem, which was something simple about free radical formation and was worth 5% of the total paper marks. "*Cool,*" they thought, "*this is going to be easy.*" They finished that problem and turned the page.

However, they were unprepared for what they saw.

The question read, 'Which wheel? (95%)'

Jumping the Gun

Teacher says, "*David, give me a sentence beginning with 'I'.*"
David replies, "*I is…*"

Teacher interrupts, "*No, David. Always say 'I am'.*"
David replies, "*Okay, I am the ninth letter of the alphabet.*"

Road to Success

A student attends a young professor's office hours.

She glances down the corridor, closes his door and kneels pleadingly. "*I would do anything to pass this exam,*" she says.

She leans closer to him, flips back her hair and gazes meaningfully into his eyes. "*I mean,*" she whispers, "*I would do anything...*"

He returns her gaze, "*Anything?*"

"*Anything.*"

His voice softens, "*Anything?*"

"*Anything,*" she repeats once again.

His voice turns to a whisper. "*Would you...study?*"

Quality Control

Skimbleshanks was in trouble again. The external examiner's comments on his second year 'Statistical Thermodynamics and Quantum Consciousness' paper had been passed directly to the Vice-Chancellor, who had called in Ms Montmorency, the Pro-Vice-Chancellor for Teaching, to investigate.

So, on a sunny spring day, Professor Skimbleshanks found himself face-to-face with Ms Montmorency. Montmorency didn't much care for Skimbleshanks and vice versa. Montmorency snapped and growled while Skimbleshanks purred – it was a literal (and literary) cat and dogfight.

The examination question was innocent enough.

Question: Is Hell exothermic or endothermic? Explain your reasoning.

It was Skimbleshanks' model answer that had given offence.

Model Answer: First, we need to establish how the mass of Hell is changing with time. So we need to know the rate at which souls are moving into Hell and the rate they are leaving.

We can safely assume that once a soul gets to Hell, it will not leave. Therefore, no souls are leaving. As for the number of souls entering Hell, we should look at the different religions that exist in the world today. Some of these state that if you are not a member of their religion, you will go to Hell. Since there are more than one of these religions and since people do not belong to more than one religion, we can project that most souls will go to Hell and we can therefore expect the number of souls in Hell to increase with time. Boyle's Law states that, in order for the temperature and pressure in Hell to stay the same, the volume of Hell must expand as souls are added.

This gives two possibilities:

(i) If Hell is expanding at a slower rate than the rate at which souls enter, then the temperature and pressure in Hell will increase until all Hell breaks loose; or

(ii) If Hell is expanding at a faster rate than the increase of souls, then the temperature and pressure will drop until Hell freezes over.

So, which is it? Here, we note the postulate provided to me by the Vice-Chancellor in his recent letter to professorial staff regarding remuneration:

"...Skimbleshanks, it will be a cold day in Hell before I give you a pay rise."

Taking into account the fact that I have not secured a salary increase in the VC's last ten pay reviews, then (ii) cannot be true and it is evident that Hell is exothermic.

Punctuation Rules

In a lesson, the professor writes the following sentence on the blackboard and tells his students to punctuate it: 'A woman without her man is nothing.'

A male student writes:

'A woman, without her man, is nothing.'

A female student writes:

'A woman: without her, man is nothing.'

Conundrum E

A professor is on holiday on an island in the South Seas that is inhabited by two tribes: one always tells the truth, while the other always lies. The professor comes to a fork in a road and has to ask a native bystander which branch he should take to reach a village. He has no way of knowing whether the native is a truth-teller or a liar. However, by asking just one question, the professor knows which road to take. What question does he ask?

LIMERICKS

A referee for the IEEE
Considers all papers with glee:
"What's new is not true,
And what's true is not new,
Unless it was written by me."

The professor was so clever and wise,
When his work was inspired by highs.
In the cosmos he'd dine
On rose-petal wine,
With giraffes wearing purple bow ties.

There was a young lady called Bright
Who could travel much faster than light.
She set out one day
In a relative way
And returned on the previous night.

A dying mosquito exclaimed,
"*A chemist has poisoned my brain.*"
The cause of his sorrow
Was para-dichloro-diphenyl-trichloroethane.

Ford did not invent the car,
The Germans were quicker by far,
But he found a way,
To make hundreds a day,
And that's how things got as they are.

Miss Farad was pretty and sensual
And charged to a reckless potential.
But a rascal named Ohm
Conducted her home.
Her decline was, alas, exponential.

There was a young fellow who thought
Very little but thought it a lot.
Then at long last he knew
What he wanted to do,
But before he could start, he forgot.

There once was a maid from Madras
Who had a magnificent ass.
Not rounded and pink,
As you'd possibly think;
It was grey, had long ears, and ate grass.

There once was a vicar at Kew
Who kept his pet cat in a pew.
He taught it to speak
Alphabetical Greek,
But it never got farther than μ.

Said an ape as he swung by his tail,
To his children both female and male,
"From your offspring, my dears,
In a couple of years,
May evolve a professor at Yale."

Conundrum F

The numbers in the diagram below are arranged according to a certain rule. Work out the rule and fill in the missing number. The number seven in the final circle is not a typographical error.

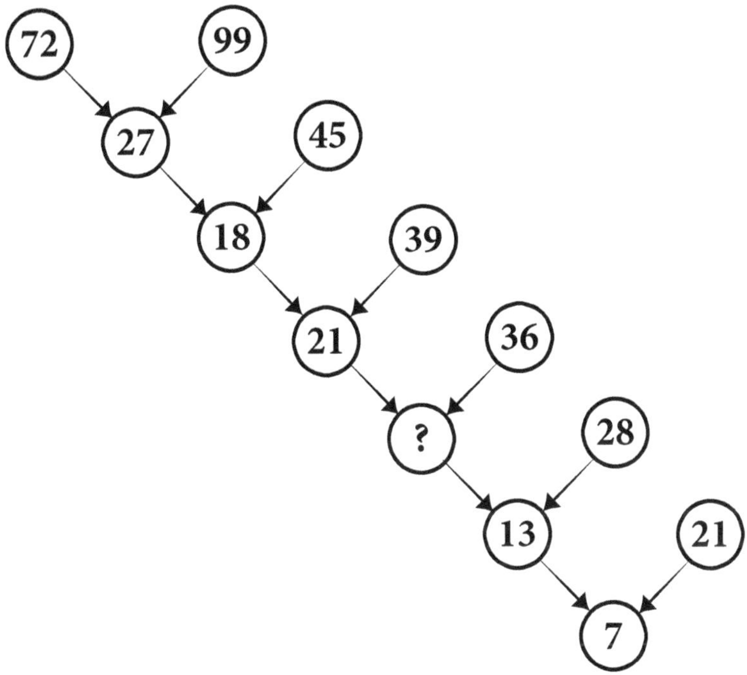

REFLECTIONS OF THE GOOD AND GREAT

We talk about it for 20 minutes and then we decide I was right.
Brian Clough on listening to players' opinions.

All women become like their mothers. That is their tragedy. No man does. That's his.
Oscar Wilde

There is only one thing in life worse than being talked about, and that is not being talked about.
Oscar Wilde

Education is an admirable thing, but it is well to remember from time to time that nothing that is worth knowing can be taught.
Oscar Wilde

If A is success in life, then A is equal to X plus Y plus Z. Work is X; Y is play; and Z is keeping your mouth shut.
Albert Einstein

Once you eliminate the impossible, whatever remains, no matter how improbable, must be the truth.
Sherlock Holmes

All truth passes through three stages. First, it is ridiculed. Second, it is violently opposed. Third, it is accepted as being self-evident.
Arthur Schopenhauer

I have never let my schooling interfere with my education.
Mark Twain

There's no beginning to your talents.
Clive Anderson (to Jeffrey Archer).

What is a cynic? A man who knows the price of everything and the value of nothing.
Oscar Wilde

In this world, nothing can be said to be certain, except death and taxes.
Benjamin Franklin

There are only two tragedies in life: one is not getting what one wants, and the other is getting it.
Oscar Wilde

Education is what remains after one has forgotten what one has learned in school.
Albert Einstein

I find television very educating. Every time somebody turns on the set, I go into the other room and read a book.
Groucho Marx

In England, we have come to rely upon a comfortable time lag of fifty years or a century intervening between the perception that something ought to be done and a serious attempt to do it.
H. G. Wells

I believe that a scientist looking at non-scientific problems is just as dumb as the next guy.
Richard P. Feynman

The actions of men are the best interpreters of their thoughts.
James Joyce

Time spent with cats is never wasted.
Sigmund Freud

Never have children, only grandchildren.
Gore Vidal

I have not failed. I've just found 10,000 ways that won't work.
Thomas A. Edison

Success consists of going from failure to failure without loss of enthusiasm.
Winston Churchill

Today you are you! That is truer than true! There is no one alive who is you-er than you!
Dr. Seuss

Conundrum G

You have an eight-litre jug full of water. You also have a five-litre jug and a three-litre jug, both empty. None of the jugs have any measurements on them. Fill one of the jugs with exactly four litres.

MEANWHILE, DOWN AT THE PUB

A man walks into a pub and orders six whiskies. He lines them up in a row and knocks back the first, third and fifth glasses. Then he gets up to leave.

"*Don't you want the others?*" asks the barman. "*You've only had three of your whiskies.*"

"*Best not,*" replies the man. "*My doctor said it was only okay to have the odd drink.*"

An infinite number of mathematicians walk into a pub. The first says, "*I'll have a pint of beer.*" The second says, "*I'll have half a pint.*" The third says, "*I'll have a quarter of a pint.*" The fourth says, "*I'll have an eighth of a pint.*"...

The landlord pulls just two pints. "*Is that all we're getting?*" ask the mathematicians. "*How do you expect us to get drunk on that?*"

The landlord replies, "*Come on guys. Know your limits.*"

A group of fonts walk into a pub. "*Get out of my pub!*" shouts the landlord, "*We don't serve your type in here.*"

The infinite number of mathematicians then walk into a different pub. The first orders a pint of beer. The second orders half a pint. The third orders a third of a pint. The fourth orders a quarter of a pint…

The landlord shouts, "*Get out of here, are you trying to ruin me?*"

A man walks into a pub and asks the barman, "*When do you finish serving?*" The barman replies, "*When I get to the 'g'.*"

An electron and a neutron go into a pub and order drinks. "*How much?*" asks the neutron. The barman replies, "*Three pounds fifty for your small friend, but for yourself, there's no charge.*"

The barman says, "*Sorry, we don't allow your kind in here.*" A tachyon walks into a pub.

A Roman walks into a pub and asks for a Martinus. "*You mean a Martini?*" the landlord asks. The Roman replies, "*If I wanted a double, I would have asked for it!*"

A man walks into a pub with a lump of tarmac under his arm. "*What would you like?*" asks the barman. The man replies, "*A pint of beer and one for the road.*"

Two chemists go into a pub. The first says, "*I think I'll have an H2O.*" The second one says, "*I think I'll have an H2O too*" – and he died.

A man goes into a pub with a newt sitting on his shoulder. "*I'll have a pint of beer and a glass of orange juice for Tiny here.*"

"*Why is he called Tiny?*" asks the barman.

The man replies, "*Because he's my newt.*"

C, E-flat and G walk into a pub. The landlord shows them the door and says, "*Sorry, we don't serve minors.*"

Schrödinger's cat walks into a pub. And doesn't.

Conundrum H

There are two vessels, one containing a litre of wine and the other a litre of water. One cubic centimetre of water is transferred to the vessel of wine and the resulting mixture is stirred thoroughly. Then a cubic centimetre of this mixture is transferred back to the vessel containing the water. Is there now more water in the wine than wine in the water? Or vice-versa?

APRIL FOOL

April Fools' Day is an annual celebration in some European and Western countries commemorated on April 1st by playing practical jokes and spreading hoaxes. The origins of this custom are somewhat obscure. Some historians speculate that April Fools' Day dates back to 1582, when France switched from the Julian calendar to the Gregorian calendar. People who were slow to get the news or failed to recognise that the start of the New Year had moved to January 1st became the butt of jokes (Poissons d'Avril). Another story is rooted in Geoffrey Chaucer's 1392 book The Canterbury Tales. In the Nun's Priest's Tale, a fox plays a prank on a rooster (who is almost eaten because of it). However, the story doesn't actually directly refer to April 1st, but to 'syn March bigan thritty dayes and two,' which has been taken by some to mean April 1st.

Here are some more recent April Fool pranks.

Spaghetti Harvest

April 1st 1957: the respected BBC news programme Panorama revealed that thanks to a very mild winter and the virtual elimination of the dreaded spaghetti weevil, Swiss farmers were enjoying a bumper spaghetti crop. The announcement was accompanied with footage of Swiss peasants pulling strands of spaghetti down from trees. Many viewers were taken in. Some called the BBC wanting to know how they could grow their own spaghetti tree. To this, the BBC diplomatically replied, '*place a sprig of spaghetti in a tin of tomato sauce and hope for the best.*' Even the Director-General of the BBC later admitted that after seeing the show, he checked in an encyclopaedia to find out if that was how spaghetti actually grew (but the encyclopaedia had no information on the topic).

Colour TV

April 1st 1962: Sweden's SVT (Sveriges Television) brought their technical expert, Kjell Stensson, onto the news to inform the public that, thanks to a new technology, viewers could convert their existing sets to colour reception. At the time, there was only the one TV channel in Sweden, and it broadcast in black and white, so this was big news. Stensson explained that all viewers had to do was pull a nylon stocking over their TV screen, and the mesh would cause the light to bend in such a way that it would appear as if the image were in colour. He proceeded to demonstrate the process. Thousands of people were fooled. Many Swedes today still report remembering their fathers rushing through the house trying to find stockings to place over the TV set. Regular colour broadcasts only commenced in Sweden on April 1st, 1970.

Write-Only Memory

April 1st 1973: The US Signetics Corporation issued a press release announcing their invention of a revolutionary new electronic memory that promised to '*improve the quality of life for billions of people who are affected by computer data.*' As opposed to the common 'Write-and-Read' or 'Read-Only' memories (ROM), they had perfected Fully-Encoded 9046XN 25120 Write-Only Memory (WOM). Data could be written to the device, but never read back, thus ensuring Eternally Inaccessible Storage (EIS). Accompanying the press release was a data sheet (written by Signetics engineer John Curtis) detailing the chip's technical specifications. Write-Only Memory became a popular joke within the electronics community, with engineers, over subsequent years, repeatedly trying to convince their managers of the need to purchase quantities of this vital component.

Decrease in Gravity

April 1st 1976: During an early-morning interview on BBC Radio 2, the astronomer Patrick Moore announced that, at 9:47 am that day, a once-in-a-lifetime astronomical event was going to occur. Pluto would pass behind Jupiter, and this planetary alignment would temporarily counteract and lessen the Earth's own gravity. Moore told his listeners that if they jumped in the air at the exact moment the alignment occurred, they would experience a strange floating sensation. At 9:47 am, the station began receiving hundreds of phone calls from listeners claiming to have felt the sensation. One woman reported that she and her friends had risen from their chairs and floated around the room. Moore had intended his announcement to be a spoof of a pseudoscientific theory that had recently been promoted in a book called The Jupiter Effect, alleging that a rare alignment of the planets was going to cause massive earthquakes and the destruction of Los Angeles in 1982.

San Serriffe

April 1st 1977: The British newspaper The Guardian published a seven-page 'special report' about San Serriffe, a small republic located in the Indian Ocean, consisting of several semi-colon-shaped islands. A series of articles described the geography and culture of this obscure nation. The report generated a huge response. The Guardian's phones rang all day as readers sought more information about the idyllic holiday spot. However, San Serriffe did not actually exist. The report was an elaborate April Fool's Day joke – one with a typographical twist, since numerous details about the island (such as its name) alluded to printer's terminology. The success of this hoax is widely credited with inspiring the British media's enthusiasm for April Foolery in subsequent years.

Big Ben Goes Digital

April 1st 1980: The BBC's overseas service reported that Big Ben was going to be given a digital readout. The news elicited a huge response from listeners shocked and angry about the change. *'Surprisingly, few people thought it was funny,'* admitted Tony Lightley of the overseas service. The same news story also claimed that the clock hands would be given away to the first four listeners to contact the station. One Japanese seaman in the mid-Atlantic immediately radioed in, hoping to be among the lucky callers.

Nixon for President – Again

April 1st 1992: National Public Radio's Talk of the Nation revealed that Richard Nixon, in a surprise move, was running for President again. His new campaign slogan was, *'I didn't do anything wrong, and I won't do it again.'* Accompanying this announcement were audio clips of Nixon delivering his candidacy speech. Listeners responded viscerally to the announcement, flooding the show with calls expressing shock and outrage. Only during the second half of the show did the host John Hockenberry reveal that the announcement was a practical joke. Nixon's voice was impersonated by comedian Rich Little.

PI Redefined

April 1st 1998: The April 1998 issue of the New Mexicans for Science and Reason newsletter contained an article claiming that the Alabama state legislature had voted to change the value of the mathematical constant pi from 3.14159 to the 'Biblical value' of 3.0. Soon the article made its way onto the internet, and then it rapidly spread around the world, forwarded by email. It only became apparent how far the article had circulated when the Alabama legislature began receiving hundreds of calls from people protesting the legislation. Physicist Mark Boslough wrote the original article, which was intended as a parody of legislative attempts to circumscribe the teaching of evolution.

The Force

April 1st 2015: Researchers at the Large Hadron Collider (LHC) confirmed the existence of The Force. In a press release, CERN's (Organisation Européenne pour la Recherche Nucléaire) Cian O'Luanaigh writes that 'new insights into the fundamental structure of the universe' were gleaned almost immediately after running the LHC at the higher energy of 13 TeV for the first time. "*The Force is what gives a particle physicist his powers,*" said a CERN theorist, 'Ben Kenobi', of the University of Mos Eisley, Tatooine. "*It's an energy field created by all living things. It surrounds us; and penetrates us; it binds the galaxy together.*" The researchers added that practical applications of the discovery include 'long-distance communication, influencing minds and lifting heavy things out of swamps.' The 570-word announcement is largely an exercise in Star Wars puns and quotes from 'dark-matter researcher Dave Vader.'

Conundrum I

A random selection of 800 twenty to thirty-year-olds living in Middlesbrough reveals 3% wearing one earring. Of the other 97%, half are wearing two earrings, half are wearing none. How many earrings altogether are being worn by this sample of the town's population?

MEDICAL MATTERS

Open Surgery

A mechanic was removing a cylinder head from a BMW M2 when he spotted a well-known cardiologist in the garage.

The cardiologist was waiting for the service manager to come and inspect his Jaguar F Type when the mechanic shouted across the garage, "*Hey Doc, come and look at this?*"

The cardiologist, a bit surprised, walked over to where the mechanic was working on the car. The mechanic straightened up, wiped his hands on a rag and asked, "*So Doc, look at this engine. I have opened its heart and am removing all the valves. I will repair any damage, and then replace them. When I finish, the car will run just like new. You and I are doing basically the same work. So, why do I make a modest £30,000 a year and you get over £200,000?*"

The cardiologist paused, smiled and leaned over, then whispered to the mechanic... "*Try doing it with the engine running.*"

No Sympathy

A vicar, an ophthalmologist and an engineer were playing a round of golf one morning behind a particularly slow group of golfers.

The engineer fumed, "*What's going on with those chaps? We must have been waiting for fifteen minutes!*"

The doctor noted, "*I don't know, but I've never seen such inept golf!*"

The vicar said, "*Here comes the green keeper. Let's have a word with him.*"

"*Hello, George. What's wrong with that group ahead of us? They're rather slow, aren't they?*"

The green keeper replied, "*Oh, yes. That's a group of blind firemen. They all lost their sight saving our clubhouse from a fire last year, so we let them play for free anytime.*"

The group fell silent for a moment. Then the vicar said, "*That's so sad. I'll say a special prayer for them.*"

The ophthalmologist added, "*Good idea. And maybe I could examine them to see if there's anything I can do for them.*"

They were again silent for a moment.

Then the engineer said, "*Why can't they play at night?*"

Seeing is Believing

An old snake goes to see his doctor. "*Doc, I need something for my eyes. I can't see very well these days.*"

The doctor prescribes a pair of spectacles and tells him to return in a fortnight's time.

The snake comes back two weeks later and tells the doctor he's now very depressed.

The doctor says, "*What's your problem? Didn't the glasses help you?*"

"*The glasses are fine, Doc, but I've just discovered I've been living with a garden hose for two years!*"

Eponymous Disorder

Man goes to the doctor. *"Doc, I can't stop singing 'The Green Green Grass of Home'."*

The doctor says, *"That sounds like Tom Jones syndrome."*

"Is it common?" the man asks.

"It's not unusual," replies the doctor.

Mistaken Diagnosis

A concerned husband goes to see the family doctor and says, *"I think my wife is deaf because she never hears me the first time I say something. In fact, I often have to repeat things over and over again."*

"*Well,*" the doctor replies, *"go home tonight, stand about 15 feet from her and say something. If she doesn't reply, move about five feet closer and say it again. Keep doing this so we can get an idea about the severity of her deafness."*

The husband returns home and does exactly as instructed. He starts off about 15 feet from his wife in the kitchen and as she is chopping some vegetables, he says, "*Darling, what's for dinner?*" He gets no response, so moves about five feet closer and asks again. No reply. He moves five feet closer. Still, no reply. He gets fed up and moves right behind her, about six inches away, and asks again, "*Darling, what's for dinner?*" His wife replies, *"For the fourth time, vegetable stew!"*

Death's Door

A man visits his doctor for a full check-up. The doctor enters, holding the results. "*I am afraid I have some very bad news,*" says the doctor. "*You don't have very long to live.*"

"*Oh, that's terrible,*" says the man. "*Exactly how long have I got?*"

"*Ten,*" the doctor says sadly.

"*Ten?*" the man asks. "*Ten what? Months? Weeks?*"

"*Nine...*"

Conundrum J

A girl arrives at a riverbank with a wolf, a goat and a bunch of cabbages. She needs to cross the river, but the one boat available can carry only her and a single item at the same time. She cannot leave the wolf alone with the goat or the goat alone with the cabbages, as, in both cases, the former will eat the latter.

How does the girl cross the river in the shortest number of journeys?

PEOPLE AND POLITICS

Lost for Words

A Yorkshire farmer's wife had recently passed away, so the farmer approached his neighbour, a wise professor, for advice on the obituary notice.

"*I thought something like, 'Mary Ackroyd, died 23rd March 2017',*" said the farmer.

"*I think you should add some more detail,*" responded the professor, "*to say how she will be missed. After all, you are paying the newspaper for 15 words.*"

A few days later, the farmer returned. "*What about: 'Mary Ackroyd, died 23rd March 2017. Sadly missed'?*"

"*Better,*" responded the professor. "*Make it a bit more personal. Say who misses her. You still have seven words left.*"

The next version came back a day later: 'Mary Ackroyd, died 23rd March 2017. Sadly missed by husband and son.'

"Almost there," came the reply. *"There are still three words you are paying for, but not using."*

The final version: 'Mary Ackroyd, died 23rd March 2017. Sadly missed by husband and son. Tractor for sale.'

Consonant Crazy

A Polish man goes to visit the optician.

"Please look at the chart on the wall," says the optician. *"Do you recognise any of the characters on the bottom line?"*

"Recognise? I went to school with them."

Confusing Consignment

Nelson Mandela is sitting at home when he hears a knock at the door. When he opens it, a Japanese man clutching a clipboard confronts him, yelling, *"You sign! You sign!"* while pointing at a lorry-load of car exhausts. Nelson says, *"Look, you've obviously got the wrong address"* and shuts the door. The next day, Nelson hears another knock at the door. When he opens it, the Japanese man is back with a lorry-load of brake pads. He shoves his clipboard under Nelson's nose, shouting, *"You sign! You sign!"* Nelson pushes the Japanese man away, saying, *"Clear off! You've got the wrong man!"* And he slams the door. The following day, the Japanese man is back again. Once again, he thrusts the clipboard under Nelson's nose, shouting, *"You sign! You sign!"* Behind him are two lorries full of windscreens. Nelson loses his temper. *"Look, I don't want these. You must have the wrong name! Who do you want to deliver these to?"* The Japanese man looks at him, puzzled, consults his clipboard and says, *"So, you not Nissan Main Dealer?"*

Blind Faith

A priest tries to survive a flood by climbing on the roof of his house. A man in a boat rows past and offers to take the priest with him. *"No thanks,"* shouts the priest, *"God will help me."* The water rises further and a man in a motorboat comes to rescue the priest. Again, he declines. *"No, thank you. God will help me."* The waters get higher still and a helicopter arrives to winch the priest to safety. *"No thanks!"* shouts the priest. *"God will surely help me."* Finally, the waters sweep over the top of the house and wash the priest into the torrent. *"God! Why has thou forsaken me?"* glugs the drowning priest. *"What do you mean 'forsaken' you?"* God shouts back. *"First, I sent a rowing boat, then a power boat, then I sent a helicopter..."*

Etiquette for a Revolving Door

It is still common practice for a man to hold the door open for a woman.

Suppose this is a revolving door? If a man and a woman are both approaching a revolving door, what is the correct protocol? Should a man let a woman go before him, or move in front of her? The problem is, if the woman goes in first, she has to push the door, but if the man goes in first, this may be deemed impolite – and there's still that last tiny bit where the woman has to push.

So, the scheme the Victorians came up with was that the man goes in first (thereby doing all the hard pushing work), but goes round one and a half times, so the woman emerges first.

Conversation with The Almighty

Man: *"God, how long is a million years?"*

God: *"To me, it's about a minute."*

Man: *"God, how much is a million pounds?"*

God: *"To me, it's a penny."*

Man: "*God, may I have a penny?*"

God: "*Wait a minute.*"

Two Rights

A linguistics professor was lecturing his class. "*In English,*" he said, "*a double negative forms a positive. However, in some languages, such as Russian or Portuguese, a double negative remains a negative. But there isn't a single language, not one, in which a double positive can express a negative.*"

A voice from the back of the room piped up, "*Yeah, right.*"

Fishy Quest

A professor arriving in Boston for a conference found that his first evening was free, so he decided to go and find a good seafood restaurant that served scrod, a Massachusetts specialty. Getting into a taxi, he asked the driver, "*Do you know where I can get scrod around here?*"

"*People ask me that all the time,*" said the taxi driver, "*but it's the first time I've heard this question in the pluperfect indicative.*"

Passport to Heaven

(In memory of the late, great Dave Allen).

One day, three men died and went to heaven. "*Religion?*" God's secretary asked the first man.

"*Jewish,*" the man replied.

"*Okay, go to room 23, but be very quiet when you go past room eight,*" the secretary said.

"*Religion?*" he asked the second man.

"Muslim."

"Go to room ten, but be very quiet when you go past room eight."

"Religion?" he asked the third man.

"Agnostic."

"Go to room 71, but be very quiet when you go past room eight."

"Why must I be quiet when I go past room eight?" the man asked.

The secretary replied, *"Oh, the Catholics are in room eight, and they think they are the only ones here."*

The Elephant and the Blind Men

The parable of the blind men and an elephant originated many years ago in the Indian subcontinent. It is a story of a group of six blind men, who have never come across an elephant before and decide to learn what the elephant is like by touching it. Each blind man feels a different part of the elephant body, but only one part, such as the leg or the tusk.

"The elephant is a pillar," said the first man, who touched his leg.

"No! It is like a rope," argued the second, after feeling the tail.

"Definitely not! An elephant is like a thick branch of a tree," the third man conjectured, after touching the trunk.

"Like an enormous hand fan," supposed the fourth man, feeling the ear.

"A huge wall," announced the fifth man, who had groped the stomach.

"It is like a solid pipe," said the sixth man, with the elephant's tusk in his hand.

The men then fell into a heated argument as to who was right in describing the big beast, all sticking to their own perception.

A wise man happened to hear the argument, stopped, and asked them what the matter was.

"We cannot agree on the nature of the elephant," they said.

The wise man then calmly replied, *"You are all both correct and incorrect. But each of you has only touched a part of the elephant's body. Therefore, you only have a restricted view of the animal. Only when you put your observations together, will you get an idea of what an elephant looks like."*

Politically Incorrect

50,000 UK Independence Party supporters meet up in a football stadium for a 'UKIP Members are Not Stupid' convention. Nigel Farage addresses the crowd, *"We are all here today to prove to the world that UKIP Members are not stupid. Can I have a volunteer please?"*

A young man keenly works his way through the crowd and steps up to the stage.

Farage asks him, *"What is 15 plus 15?"*

After 15 or 20 seconds, the man says, *"Eighteen!"*

Obviously everyone is a little disappointed. Then the UKIP Members start chanting, *"Give him another chance! Give him another chance!"*

Farage says *"Well, since we have a capacity crowd, world-wide press and global broadcast media here, I think we can give him another chance."*

So he asks, *"What is five plus five?"*

After nearly 30 seconds, the man eventually says, *"Ninety?"*

Farage looks down and just lets out a dejected sigh. Everyone is disheartened.

But then the 50,000 supporters begin to yell and wave their hands shouting, *"GIVE HIM ANOTHER CHANCE! GIVE HIM ANOTHER CHANCE!"*

Farage, unsure whether he is now doing more harm than good, eventually says,

"What is two plus two?"

Silence hangs over the gathering.

The young man closes his eyes, and after a whole minute, eventually says,

"Four??????"

Pandemonium breaks out throughout the stadium as the UKIP crowd stand to a man, wave their arms, stomp their feet and scream…

"*GIVE HIM ANOTHER CHANCE! GIVE HIM ANOTHER CHANCE!*"

Reason for Brexit?

The European Commission has announced an agreement whereby English will be the official language of the EU, rather than German, which was the other contender. Her Majesty's Government conceded that English spelling has room for improvement and has therefore accepted a five-year phasing in of 'Euro-English.'

In the first year, 's' will replace the soft 'c.' Sertainly, this will make sivil servants jump for joy. The hard 'c' will be dropped in favour of the 'k,' which should klear up some konfusion and allow one key less on keyboards.

There will be growing publik enthusiasm in the sekond year, when the troublesome 'ph' will be replaced with 'f,' making words like 'fotograf' 20% shorter.

In the third year, publik akseptanse of the new spelling kan be expekted to reach the stage where more komplikated changes are possible. Governments will enkourage the removal of double letters, which have always ben a deterent to akurate speling. Also, al wil agre that the horible mes of the silent 'e' is disgrasful.

By the fourth yer, peopl wil be reseptiv to steps such as replasing 'th' with 'z' and 'w' with 'v.'

During ze fifz yer, ze unesesary 'o' kan be dropd from vords kontaining 'ou' and similar changes vud of kors be aplid to ozer kombinations of leters. After zis fifz yer, ve vil hav a reli sensibl riten styl. Zer vil be no mor trubls or difikultis and everivun vil find it ezi to understand ech ozer. ZE DREM VIL FINALI COM TRU!

Conundrum K

A pile of potatoes weighing 100 kg is put in the sun. 99% of the weight of potatoes is made up of water. After a day, some of the water evaporates, with the result that 98% of the potatoes is now made up of water. What is the new weight of the potatoes?

CONUNDRUMS EXPLAINED

Conundrum A

The answer to this puzzle is a simple matter of the Metro timetable. While the Newcastle and North Shields trains arrive equally often – at ten-minute intervals – their schedules are such that the Newcastle train always arrives one minute after the North Shields train. Thus, the Newcastle train will be the first to arrive only if the student happens to arrive at the station during this one-minute interval. If she arrives at any other time, i.e. during a nine-minute interval, the North Shields train will come first. Since the girl's arrival at the station is random, the odds are nine to one for the boyfriend in North Shields.

Conundrum B

There is only one guest, as shown in the family tree below:

The Dean's father is Mr C, so the guest is the Dean's father's brother-in-law. Similarly, each of the other descriptions of the guest represents a different path from the Dean to him: via the Dean's brother (Mr E), via his father-in-law (Mr B) and via his brother-in-law (Mr D).

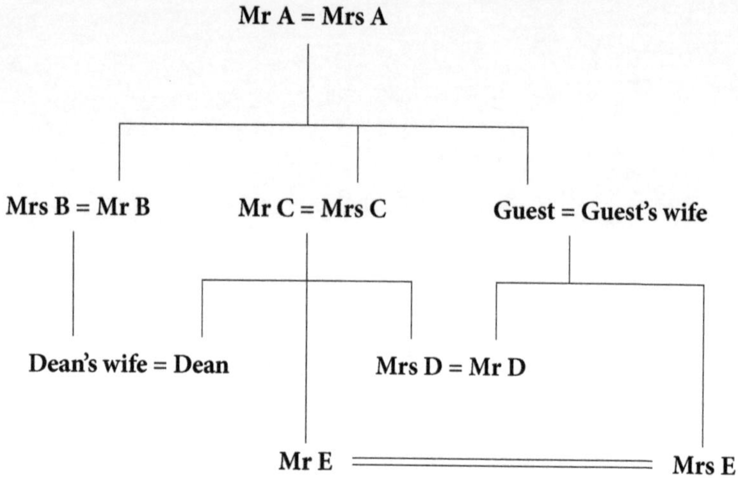

Conundrum C

The player who goes first will always win, if he or she applies the following strategy:

Player 1 places the first coin dead centre on the table. In all subsequent moves, he or she simply places a coin in the opposite position to where Player 2 has just played. Since the table starts empty, wherever Player 2 places a coin, it will always be possible for Player 1 to put a coin in the opposite position. So, Player 1 cannot lose and eventually Player 2 will find no free table left on which to place a coin.

Conundrum D

Multiplication of the three children's ages gives 36. The following are possibilities. The final column shows the sum of the ages.

Ages			Product	Sum
1	1	36	36	38
1	2	18	36	21
1	4	9	36	14
1	6	6	36	13
2	2	9	36	13
2	3	6	36	11
3	1	12	36	16
3	3	4	36	10

Assume that the vicar knows, or can find out, the number on the verger's door. If the door number was the same as a number that appears only once in the final column of the table above, the vicar would immediately know the ages of the children. But, if the door number is 13, he would require more information. So, the ages are either

1,6,6 or 2,2,9

The vicar obviously knows the age of his son and it is assumed that the verger does too. Since the verger has told the vicar that this piece of information is sufficient to determine the ages, the vicar's son must be older than all the children in one set of possible ages, but younger than at least one child in the other possible set of ages. In other words, the vicar's son must be either 7 or 8. If the vicar's son was, say, 10 or 11, then since the son would be older than all the children in both possibilities, the verger would not have been able to state that the vicar could solve the problem. And if the vicar's son is 7 or 8, the verger's children are 1, 6 and 6.

Conundrum E

If an answer of 'Yes' or 'No' is required, there are several questions that might be asked, all using the same logic.

For example, the professor points to one of the roads and asks, "*If I were to ask you if this road leads to the village, would you say 'Yes'?*" The native is then forced to give the correct answer, even if he is a liar. If the road does lead to the village, the liar would say *'No'* to the direct question. However, as the question is put, he would lie and would respond *'Yes.'* On the other hand, if the road actually does not go to the village, the liar is forced in the same way to reply *'No'* to the professor's question.

A similar question would be, "*If I asked a member of the other tribe whether this road leads to the village, would he say 'Yes'?*"

Conundrum F

One's eye is drawn to the top left. How can 72 and 99 make 27?

This seems straightforward

$$99 - 72 = 27$$

The same pattern follows for the 18 in the next circle

$$45 - 27 = 18$$

This subtraction seems to work, suggesting the missing number is the difference between 36 and 21.

$$36 - 21 = 13$$

HOWEVER, when the circled 7 is reached, this is NOT the difference between 21 and 13.

Clearly, another rule is at work.

Going back to the top left

$$7 + 2 + 9 + 9 = 27$$

This works for ALL the other lines

$$2 + 7 + 4 + 5 = 18$$

The missing number is therefore

$$2 + 1 + 3 + 6 = 12$$

Conundrum G

Call the five-litre jug A and the three-litre jug B.

A and B start empty.

Fill A up. The states of the jugs are now: A = 5; B = 0.

Now pour A into B. The states are now: A = 2; B = 3.

Empty B into the 3rd jug: A = 2; B = 0.

Pour A into B: A = 0; B = 2.

Fill up A again: A = 5; B = 2.

Pour A into B: A = 4; B = 3.

Jug A therefore has exactly four litres, as required.

Conundrum H

The answer is that the two quantities are exactly the same. This can be illustrated by representing the wine and water with, say, 100 red and 100 white marbles, respectively.

If 25, say, red marbles are mixed in with the white marbles, and 25 marbles of any colour are returned to the red container, then there will again be 100 marbles in each container. If there are now x white marbles in the red container, then there must be x red marbles in the white container. The mixtures will therefore be of equal purity.

(Intermolecular forces between the water and wine molecules will result in the volume of the mixture of wine and water being very slightly less than the sum of the two original volumes. However, the above result is correct as a first approximation).

Conundrum I

Among the 97%, if half wear two earrings and half none, this is the same as if each person wore one. Assuming, then, that each of the 800 people sampled is wearing one earring, there are 800 earrings in all.

Conundrum J

Start with the student on the left bank. She begins with three items and can only take one of them on the boat. If she takes the wolf, the goat will be left with the cabbages and eat them. If she takes the cabbages, the wolf will eat the goat. By a process of elimination, the only item she can take on the first crossing is the goat, since wolves don't eat cabbages. She delivers the goat to the right bank and returns for the next item.

Now, the student has a choice of wolf or cabbages. Assume she decides to take the cabbages. She crosses the river for the third time. When she reaches the right bank, she cannot leave the cabbages with the goat, so what does she do? She makes no progress if she returns with the cabbages, since she only just arrived with them, so she must return with the goat. Back on the left bank, after four crossings, the student chains the goat and departs for her fifth journey with the wolf. On the right bank, the wolf remains uninterested in the cabbages. All that remains is one trip back to pick up the goat and the task is completed in seven crossings.

(There's a second, equivalent solution: with the student taking the wolf on the second crossing).

Conundrum K

The answer is 50 kg. The potatoes lose half their weight! This answer can be calculated as follows:

Water makes up 99% of potatoes. Hence, the remaining 1% is potato 'essence.' The ratio of potato essence to water is 1 to 99. After evaporation, only 98% of the potatoes is water, so the ratio of potato essence to water becomes 2 to 98, which is the same ratio as 1 to 49. Since the amount of potato essence remains at 1 kg, the amount of water must reduce to 49 kg, so the total weight of the potatoes is 1 kg + 49 kg = 50 kg.

Milton Keynes UK
Ingram Content Group UK Ltd.
UKHW011847071223
433930UK00002B/7

9 781999 603908